The Dieter's Guide To Weight Loss During Sex

by Richard Smith

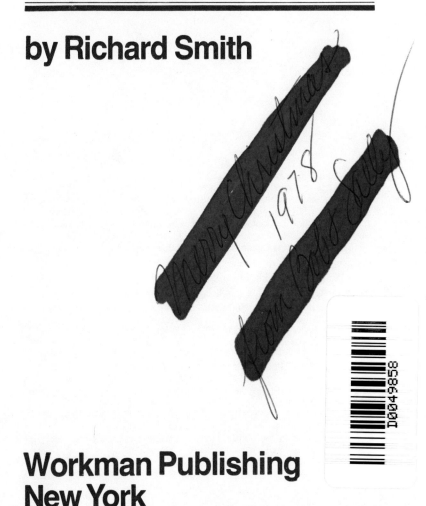

Workman Publishing
New York

Acknowledgment

There are many to whom I am indebted, but they wish, alas, to remain anonymous.

Library of Congress Cataloging in Publication Data

Smith, Richard.
     The dieter's guide to weight loss during sex.

     1. Sex—Anecdotes, facetiae, satire, etc.
2. Reducing—Anecdotes, facetiae, satire, etc.
I. Title.
PN6231.S54S57   818'.5'407   77-18424
ISBN 0-89480-023-X

Jacket design: Paul Hanson

Workman Publishing Company
1 West 39th Street
New York, New York 10018

Manufactured in the United States of America
First printing April 1978
10 9 8 7 6 5 4 3 2

Contents

Introduction 7

I. Preparing for Your Partner

Physical Conditioning 13
Basic Exercises.....................................14
Mental Conditioning 17
Personal Grooming..................................18

II. Setting the Scene and Initial Intimacy

Preparing the Bedroom 21
Preparing the Bathroom 22
Additional Last-Minute Preparations 23
Getting Partner in Mood and Alerting Mutual
    Sensibilities 24
Communicating 26
Making the First Move 28
Overcoming Resistance 29
Body Contact and Initial Touching 30
Kissing 31
Removing Clothes..................................32
Arousal and Stimulation (advanced) 34
Weight Loss Bonus #1 35
Weight Loss Bonus #2 36
Embarrassment 37
Disappointment 38
Getting into Bed 40

III. Foreplay

Ten Alternate Erogenous Zones 42
Being Good in Bed 43

Being Even Better in Bed 45
Going Too Far 46
Writhing 47
Teasing 48
Stroking 49
Oral Sex 50
Removing Hair...................................51
Disposing of Hair 52
Achieving Erection 53
Sustaining Erection 54
Weight Loss Bonus #3 55
Putting on Prophylactic 56
Inserting Diaphragm 57
Delays..58
Further Delays 59
Emotional Distress 60

IV. Intercourse and Things Related

Doing It for the First Time 62
Doing It for the Last Time 63
Doing It 64
Insertion 65
Satisfying Partner................................67
Positions 68
Positions (According to Nationality) 70
Locations 71
Intercourse 72
Possible Side Effects of Intercourse 73
Sex-Related Noises 74
Seeking Comfort 75
Approaching Orgasm 76
Orgasm 77
Orgasmic Intensity Scale.........................78
Pulling Out 79
Multiple Orgasms for Female 80
Multiple Orgams for Male 81
Special Orgasms 82

Premature Ejaculation 83
Consequences of Premature Ejaculation
    for Female 84
Consequences of Premature Ejaculation
    for Male 85
Achieving Orgasm Under Unusual Circumstances ...86
Delaying Orgasm 87

V. Afterward

Weight Loss Bonus #4 90
Things Often Said After Sex 91
Possible Side Effects of Good Sex 92
Possible Side Effect of Bad Sex 93
Recovering 94
Rolling Over and Going to Sleep....................95
Sleep 96
Trying Again......................................97
Tidying and Cleaning Up 98
Showering 99
Drying Off..100
Making the Bed 101

VI. Supplementary Activities

Male Fantasies 104
Female Fantasies..................................105
Dreaming 106
Group Sex..107
Masturbation 108
Fetishism 110
Bondage..111
Discipline 112
Whipping 113
Weight Loss Bonus #5 114
Sex with Animals 115
Bizarre Sex Practices 116

Gay Sex 117
Additional Erotic Experiences 118
Keeping a Journal 119

VII. Miscellaneous Problems, Emergencies and Disasters

Penis Envy 122
Typical Sex-Related Fears 123
Personal Fears 124
Guilt 125
Aggravation 126
More Aggravation.................................127
Acquiring Bedsores 128
Getting Caught 129
Almost Getting Caught............................130
Threatening Situations 131
Interruptions and Distractions 132
Afflictions 133
Call of Nature 134
Fighting off Pets.................................135
Assorted Accidents 136

VIII. Eating and Sex (The Bedside Eater)

Calories in Foods 139
Typical Effects of Alcohol on Bedroom Behavior 147
Examples of Weight Lost While Eating 148
Weight Lost While Resisting Food 150
Eating in Bed—Problems 151
Alternate Uses of Food 152

The Height Report

How Tall Should the Ideal Sex Partner Be?.........155

Introduction

"If you like exercise, you will like this book. If you loathe exercise, you will love this book." ANONYMOUS

How much weight do we lose during sex? Although the diet literature abounds with charts and books explaining how many calories we burn while jogging, playing tennis or golfing, similar information concerning sexual activity has, until now, been largely unavailable. Yet, a random survey of 206 million Americans indicates that 98 percent devote more time and effort to sex than to jogging, tennis or golf, and we felt the time right for a book explaining why.

In the past, efforts to determine weight loss during sex usually met with failure, possibly due to the ignorance of researchers and their poor choice of subjects. One experiment, for example, to determine calories burned during foreplay, ended abruptly when both participants fell asleep, their mutual lack of interest attributable to a fifty-six-year age difference. Another misguided experiment, an attempt to prove that regular sexual activity (a minimum of 74.2 times a week) could tighten the waistline and perk up one's tennis game collapsed when on the fourth day of the experiment, the battered participants went insane. As a result, the lack of reliable data made it impossible for the average person to calculate weight loss while removing clothing, fumbling around or attempting a truly satisfying orgasm in an unheated tent.

With few exceptions, sex is considered to be the least boring and most pleasurable form of physical exercise, not to mention the cheapest. Indeed, those who indulge have nothing but praise for its all-around benefits and vigorous endorsements such as, "I like it" . . . "It's nice" . . . "It beats walking to Uruguay in moccasins," are not uncommon. Standard exercises, of course, are effective weight-shedders but they take a good deal of time. One hour of jogging, for example, burns only six hundred calories; one hour of swimming, five hundred calories (more if you remain underwater); and two hours of pitch 'n' putt only seventy-one. On the other hand, faking an orgasm convincingly can burn as many as one hundred sixty calories in just nineteen seconds, not counting the warm-up. Add to this another twenty calories for avoiding the wet spot and thirty calories for getting a towel and the benefits of sexual activity become obvious—everything we do burns calories and two hours of enthusiastic sex can easily burn off a pastrami sandwich, a slice of pecan pie, two scoops of ice cream and those few maverick cellulites on your upper thigh. Thus, by thinking of sexual activity in terms of calories burned, we can calculate how much weight we lose, using thirty-five hundred calories to the pound. The more activity, of course, the more weight lost.

In this handbook, we have attempted to cover every conceivable aspect of sex, thereby showing you at a glance the dramatic impact chronic sexual activity has not only on the body, but on the mind as well. Although the most modern scientific methods have been used to ensure accuracy, the problems confronted were, to say the least, profound. The calories burned, for example, while trying to find a more comfortable position, will vary greatly according to whether you are comfortably ensconced on a king-size bed or scrunched in the back of a Japanese sedan. Furthermore, despite the wonders of the electronic age, the task of translating emotional reactions such as rage, disappointment, herpes and anxiety into calories-burned was such that careful estimates had to do. And finally, during the heat of passion, despite the fact that the electrodes would constantly fall off, the frenzied participants simply refused to stop and our figures had to be adjusted accordingly.

We therefore suggest that you use this book as an informal guide rather than a rigid manual, making necessary caloric adjustments according to your own individual size and temperament, plus the length of time you indulge, how you indulge and whether or not you have a partner. Once you have reached your ideal height and weight, you may still continue sexual activity without worrying about adverse side effects such as brooding or excessive slimness.

The ability of sexual activity to induce weight loss is perhaps best illustrated by the fact that one hour of heavy petting, including squirming, wiggling and whimpering for more, can easily burn off the caloric equivalent of either five shots of Creme de Menthe or a double portion of birthday cake. See the following chart for additional examples.

Sexual Activity	Burns off
1 hour of intensive foreplay (114 breaths per minute) or 18 minutes of intercourse	1 slice (large) of chocolate cake
26 minutes of nonstop intercourse plus one 9-minute orgasm, or the equivalent	2 slices of pizza with extra cheese, meatballs and mushrooms
16 minutes of frisking and tickling partner	9 lollipops
53 minutes of French kissing or 25 minutes of normal foreplay or 6 minutes of abnormal foreplay	1 cheeseburger with 14 french fries and a dollop of ketchup
2 hours of bondage or 47 minutes of flogging using a medium-weight flog	2 bottles of beer, large portion of spaghetti and 1 slice of toast

7 minutes of aural sex (anything involving partner's ear)	6 Hershey Kisses (no tinfoil)
15 minutes of oral sex	11 grapes
52 minutes of massaging partner's back or 10 minutes of massaging your own back	1 wedge of crab quiche Lorraine with 1 glass of wine
1 hour of stomach to stomach resuscitation	1 piece of fudge (generous)
62 minutes of chasing partner around the room at a medium jog, or a 2-hour pillow fight with 20-pound pillows	1 pint of ice cream
1 sneeze	12 bean sprouts (salted)
14 minutes of fondling	Chocolate mousse: stingy portion
Intercourse in at least 4 different positions within 6 minutes	Chocolate mousse: huge portion
31 minutes of foreplay in the lotus position	2 Cornish pasties with wild rice and pudding
24 minutes of mutually satisfying oral sex in a swimming pool	1 large slice of cheesecake

I. Preparing for Your Partner

The road to perfect sex begins with a perfect you. In addition to showing how much weight you lose while preparing for your partner, this section is designed to help you make sure that you are physically and mentally ready for even the most grueling sexual activity. For your guidance, we have listed below some questions frequently asked by people about to have sex. Use the information in the following pages to resolve any problems.

- Am I strong enough?
- Do I doubt my ability to satisfy?
- Does my heart pound just from fluffing up the pillows?
- Am I satisfied with my biceps? triceps? quadriceps? eyesight?
- Can I carry my partner into the bedroom without making a fool of myself?
- How's my complexion?
- All pimples well hidden?
- Are my toenails a sight? Are my toes aligned?
- Is anxiety causing lower abdominal distress?
- Should I eat now, or later?
- Should I take a Valium?
- Do I really need this?
- Will it be fun?
- Will it be meaningful?
- If it's meaningful, will it still be fun?

Physical Conditioning

"A sound mind in a fat body slips around."
M. TITO FARTSEK, PH.D.

It is during sex that our bodies do, or at least try to do, the most magical and wonderful things. We grab and grope, slide and squirm, reach and stretch, strain our muscles and perform feats of agility that would flabbergast an ape. Yet, instead of adequately preparing ourselves for such fervent activity, most of us think nothing of just jumping into bed without so much as a push-up, touching the toes or hopping up and down.

Along with ligament problems, this lack of preparation can lead to premature exhaustion, the first signs of which are shortness of breath, a feeling of dizziness if you lie down too fast, failure to respond to partner's strokes and an intense desire to do nothing but stare at television. And all this after just four minutes of foreplay. The result will be a sense of inadequacy and profound lethargy, a condition that may persist for as little as two hours or as long as several days, during which time it may be difficult to walk, pour juice and chew inexpensive cuts of meat. In addition, the habitually sedentary, especially those with a chronic aversion to exercise, will, in all likelihood, experience a massive charley horse.

It is obvious that being out of shape can ruin, even wreck, and possibly destroy one's sex life. According to the President's Council on Physical Fitness, a need to nap after heavy exertion such as running up an inclined surface, orgasm or making stew suggests that one's condition is less than tip-top and an exercise program might be in order.

The following modest exercises, while by no means representing a total conditioning program, will prove helpful in overcoming sexual inertia, improving virtuosity and building the stamina to cope with any partner, no matter where or how well they were trained.

Basic Exercises

(Each exercise to be performed at least one hour before sex)

Activity   **Calories burned**

Push-ups (five) 14
    General strength, firms upper arms and
    shoulders, increases ability to hold on when
    on top of partner, also makes it easier to
    remove a partner who has fainted on
    top of you.

Sit-ups (five) 10
    Tones and strengthens vital stomach
    muscles, enabling you to quickly leap out of
    bed should something go wrong. Also
    makes sitting up in bed easier should you
    wish to eat, watch television or glance at
    the time.

Reverse sit-ups (three) 563
    For super strength. Do exactly what you
    would do for a regular sit-up except lie face
    down on the floor.

Touch toes (ten) 7
    Smashes fat deposits, increases flexibility.
    Permits you to dabble with positions that
    would normally damage your spine. Also
    lets you reach for things such as food and
    sedatives without straining.

Touch waist (ten) ....½
    For those not yet loose enough to reach all
    the way to their toes. Similar effect as
    above but less—far less.

Arm curls (five, using comfortable weight) 9
    Builds strong biceps, inspires confidence
    and occasionally makes vaccination mark
    more prominent. A must for those who wish
    to lift their partner at the crucial moment
    and gallantly carry them into the bedroom.
    Without this exercise, instead of confidently
    lifting your partner, it is likely that you will
    fall to the floor and begin groaning
    piteously. This exercise is especially useful
    to the understrength woman with spindly
    arms who'd like to beat her partner at arm
    wrestling.

Squeezing a rubber ball (twenty squeezes) 3
    During sex, a strong grip is needed for
    everything from extending a hearty
    handshake to picking up fruit. It is
    especially vital for clinging to your partner
    should things get really good. For the
    woman who wants to win skirmishes or
    have her partner in her power during
    tickling sessions, a secure grip is essential.

Jogging (at least one mile).........................100
    The ultimate all-around exercise for
    increasing stamina and firming many of the
    muscles used during sex. Also enlarges
    lung capacity and increases oxygen
    efficiency, allowing you to hold your breath
    (should you have to) for prolonged periods
    of time.

The following exercises are optional.

Handstand 40
Difficult, but most rewarding. Keeping
knees straight, bend over from the waist
and place palms flat on the floor. Take two
small steps forward. You should now be
standing on your hands. Hold for the count
of ten.

Floor touch 50
Stand with arms at sides. Without bending
knees or moving feet, slowly and gracefully
lean forward and touch forehead to the
floor. Remain there, count to two, and
return to original position. Those with yoga
training will have little trouble.

Side bend 20
Clasp hands behind neck and drop to
knees. Slowly bend sideways and touch
right shoulder to floor. Remain ten seconds,
then return to original position. Repeat for
left shoulder.

There are, of course, additional methods of achieving erotic fitness. These include such vigorous exercise as tennis, skiing, bicycling, backgammon and sleeping on a cot. All are excellent for increasing cardiorespiratory endurance and perking up one's sexual performance.

Mental Conditioning

It is impossible to enjoy sex if depressed, not in the mood or the mind is distracted by everyday cares. For now, you must strive for a feeling of well-being; worries about stock losses, overdue dental bills and a grievously ill plant must be put aside. The following are common methods of cleansing the mind, dissipating tension and achieving serenity.

Activity	Calories burned
Transcendental meditation	4
Incidental meditation *(takes less time—can be done while brushing teeth)*	1
Self hypnosis	9
Psychoanalysis (per session)	17
If analyst makes house calls	12
Prayer	5
Watching an X-rated movie If it's a grainy print and you have to squint, add three calories. If the sound track is blurred and you have to put forth extra effort to hear, that's another two calories.	7
Calling a parent	3
Frisking a ham (to help get you in the mood)	3
Biofeedback If you don't have the proper equipment, just plug your fingers into your ears and listen to your hands. It really works!	6

Personal Grooming

Activity	Calories burned
Showering	8
Taking a bath	6

Drying hair
    With towel (vigorously) 9
    Blow drying 3
    Using cheeks 348
      (deduct 4.96 calories if bald)

Brushing teeth 2
With electric toothbrush .... ¼

Inspecting face for pimples, blemishes, etc. 2
    (Includes paranoiac reaction to grape-size zit
    about to debut on bridge of the nose.)

Shaving (either sex) 3

Applying cosmetics (either sex) 3

Selecting clothing
    If you care 7
    If you don't 1

II. Setting the Scene and Initial Intimacy

Creating an atmosphere of intimacy and comfort will immediately put your partner at ease and in the mood for sex. Ambiance, therefore, is everything. If you have a fireplace, light it. If it's August, don't. Check the bed. Is it strong enough? In good repair? Any joints need regluing? Is the kitty litter changed? Has the dog been gently chloroformed? Children all gone to Aunt Mabel's? Any threatening photos in view? Parrot gagged? Record albums ready? Refrigerator stocked? Plenty of ice? Bathroom looking its best? Sure, it's a lot of trouble. But the result will be a satisfied partner who will willingly and without complaint take the garbage on the way out.

Preparing the Bedroom

Activity	Calories burned

If you're fussy 42
(Give or take three calories)

    Includes dusting, fluffing up the pillows, tuning the radio, bouncing up and down on the bed, putting up posters and setting the snooze alarm. Make sure the lighting is right—too dark and the place becomes a coal mine; too light and it looks like an operating room. Try a 25-watt candle. Avoid assertive incense. Use props such as books to make a good impression and show what kind of person you are. Books of poetry, for instance, convey literacy and sensitivity. They should be conspicuously placed—on the dresser, by the night table and perhaps one or two under the covers. Besides poetry, select a few books that give the impression that you are unusual—slightly eccentric but not quite certifiable—thus adding to the mystery of the sexual experience. A few suggested titles: *Remedial Norwegian, The Romance of Welding* (Vol. II), *Build Your Own Mailbox, Jingles of the Japanese* (for those who like Haiku) and *Happy Porkchops, The Story of a Cheerful Butcher.*

Note: If someone extra special is coming, you may want to change the sheets, or at least flip them over. Add another four calories for either activity.

Preparing the Bathroom

Even under normal everyday circumstances, the bathroom should be regarded as a holy place, a sanctuary for cleansing the body, renewing the spirit and occasionally hiding from the world. During sex, however, the bathroom also becomes a first aid station. It should therefore be spotless, sparkling and filled with such amenities as soft, fluffy towels, a cheerful shower curtain, a new bar of soap with a muted aroma, an extra toothbrush and a toilet that flushes with a soothing pleasant whoosh. If possible, we suggest boiling the entire bathroom, just to be certain. If this is not convenient, see the following:

Activity	Calories burned
Erasing two-month-old ring from tub	11
Scrubbing (de-crudding) tiles	14
Removing alien vegetation from shower curtain	12
Replacing towels	3
Installing new roll of toilet paper Security is a fresh roll of toilet paper in the dispenser plus five backup rolls.	2
Scraping excessive soap buildup from soap dish	4
Disinfecting bath mat	6
Tidying medicine chest Will prevent hundreds of jars, bottles and brushes from crashing into the sink when partner gets aspirin.	3
Hiding other toothbrush	1

Additional Last-Minute Preparations

Activity	Calories burned
Vacuuming	6
Hiding sex manual	3

(If you're still not sure of what to do, write the answers on your cuffs.)

Decanting wine	4
If you don't have a corkscrew	268

(Not only does this process allow the wine to breathe, but it prevents your partner from discovering that your modest—but acutely drinkable—Bordeaux only cost $1.49, including the bottle.)

Putting on CHICKEN INSPECTOR button	1

Getting Partner in Mood and Alerting Mutual Sensibilities

(Wait until your partner arrives before commencing any of the following.)

Activity	Calories burned

Reciting poetry
    Shelley (Percy Bysshe) 3
    Lord Byron 3½
    Rossetti 4
    Milton 8
        (avoid if you have a southern accent)
    Berryman 12
    McKuen ....½

Reading *War and Peace* aloud (no rest stops) 1573

Practical jokes (a good change of pace)
    Whoopie cushion 11
    Squirting flower 14
    Fake teeth....................................7
    Joy buzzer 10
    Exploding cigar 20

All of the above are not only in impeccable taste, but great for breaking the ice.

Ribald jokes
    Dirty...8
    Filthy...14

Listening to music
Light classical 3
Heavy classical 5
Chamber music 10
Opera: Mozart 15
Verdi 27
Wagner 248
Muzak 20
Cole Porter 8
Country and western 40
Rock 93
Your own singing: good voice 18
bad voice .64
Playing the guitar (per strum) . . . . .¼
Playing a trumpet (one song) 26
(without a mouthpiece) 320

To all categories above add five calories if tapping feet.

Dancing
Fox trot 7
Minuet 9
Waltz 30
Tango: bareheaded 14
wearing wide-brimmed hat 14½
Highland fling 86

Dancing close together is a good way to get a sneak pre-
view of your partner's body tone and decide if you wish to
go any further.

Showing a silent horror film while dressed in rubber
knickers and a strange hat 18
*(slightly kinky, check with your partner before
renting a projector)*

Reading the Bible together 10

Playing doctor 8

Communicating

Activity	Calories burned

Meaningful conversation ....see below

Naturally, the shorter and less imaginative the conversation, the less energy used and the fewer calories burned. Beginning a conversation with, "I've got nothing to talk about, let's go to bed," though certainly direct, burns only three calories and may alienate the most willing partner. The longer and deeper the conversation, however, the harder your imagination works and the more calories consumed. A discussion of camel pasturalism in New Jersey or Einstein's paper on emotional distress in birds can burn as many as fifty calories and make you feel important. See the following topic suggestions for substantial caloric consumption.

Wishing rickets on your boss 24

How you are striving to become your own person 28

How you are striving to become the person your parents mean you to be 35

How you are trying to become less dependent on your: mother/father/niece/butcher....................57

All of the above 268

The echoes of Nietzsche in "Jingle Bells" 75
 (light philosophy is always surefire)

Spelling Nietzsche correctly without looking it up ...92

Should science attempt to put a man on the sun?.....60

Is it moral to drive while fully asleep? 33

Zen Buddhism and Lo Mein:
     Which is more fulfilling? 37
     Which is more filling? 40

Why love without sex is meaningless 45

Why sex without love can be pretty good..............2

Convincing partner that it is not just a
physical attraction 70

Making the First Move

Activity	Calories burned
If you are shy	15
If you have a morbid fear of success	22
If you are easily intimidated when a person acts distant and reserved A person who orders you to keep your hands to yourself is acting distant and reserved.	36
If you are an anxious person with a large inferiority complex	45
If you sell used cars	2
If you politely ask your partner if it's okay to put your arm around him/her *(so ridiculous that it sometimes works)*	17
If you beg	25

According to psychologists, the anxiety produced by the prospect of making the first move, for either sex, is directly proportional to one's fear of asking a delicatessen waiter for a clean glass.

Overcoming Resistance

Activity   **Calories burned**

Passive 1½
    Passive resistance indicated if partner,
    while trembling, utters "don't" in a low,
    meek voice. "Please don't stop" indicates
    extremely passive resistance.

Active 62
    Active resistance may include biting,
    punching and weapons. Press on if you
    think it's only an act.

Seducing partner (only applies to venal partners)
    If you are rich 5
    If you are poor 164

Body Contact and Initial Touching

Activity	Calories burned
Fumbling	4
Casually rummaging around	7
Gentle rubbing	10
Serious fondling	14
Involved massaging	17
Caressing	19
Petting Above the waist under loose-fitting garment such as sweater or raincoat Below the waist under tight ski pants *(stop if the waistband cuts off your circulation)*	 21 46
Squeezing (any part of body except entire head)	15

Kissing

Activity	Calories burned
Gentle	10
Heavy	17
Passionate	26

(Giving partner's shirt collar a hickey, for example.)

Actually sucking blood	41
Recovering shape of nose	11

French kissing
With mouth open	18
With mouth closed	239
Tongue strain	65

Dutch kissing (applies only if you're Dutch)	24

Kissing various areas of body
Uvula	11
Soft palate	9
Eyelid	3
Retina	8
Liver	37
Lungs	30
Back of nose	66
Wrist	12
Watch	10

Removing Clothes

Activity	Calories burned
With partner's consent	12

Without partner's consent	187

In winter 25
    Calorie count provides for removal of typical
    cold-weather gear—ski parka, shirt, pants,
    hat, earmuffs, scarf, gloves, long underwear,
    goggles, socks and boots.

In summer 3

Miscellaneous

Removing socks by violently shaking feet 418
    *(Very impractical and seldom works, but for
    those interested in high weight loss, it's
    essential.)*

Unhooking bra
    Using two calm hands 7
    Using one trembling hand 96
    *(The record here for incompetence is two and
    a half hours and a badly mutilated index finger.)*

Any attempt to remove panty hose without
first removing slacks 375
    *(Add another one hundred calories if you are
    actually successful.)*

Should you remove all of your clothes? The answer is generally yes, since most people take it as a sign of commitment. Women are especially put off by men who keep their socks on and also by men who, being unduly obsessed with hygiene, refuse to have sex unless permitted to keep their shorts on. There are also those who find it difficult to even temporarily part with a lucky charm, and it is not unusual for people to have sex while clutching a rabbit's foot or portable radio. It is, however, generally acceptable to wear adornments to bed such as earrings, rings, crosses, Jewish stars, ankhs and perfume.

Arousal and Stimulation (advanced)

It was difficult to assign caloric values in this category, since what is high-kilowatt sex for some may be total boredom for others. One person, for instance, may respond sexually to a pork chop; another, instead, may eat it. And there are those who do not consider the phrase "urban renewal" erotic. We therefore freely admit that the counts below are somewhat imprecise.

Activity	Calories burned
Blowing in partner's ear	
Using mouth	9
Using bellows	14
Using blow dryer (low setting)	2
Blowing in your own ear	158
(Experimental form of autoeroticism still not completely tested)	
Nibbling on partner's earlobe	8
(If your partner is a gypsy, be careful not to swallow an earring)	
Biting partner's head	27
Lust	15
Talking dirty	8

Weight Loss Bonus #1

Activity	Calories burned
Striptease	55

If you are even marginally graceful, stripping to music presents an excellent opportunity to lose weight while arousing your appreciative and leering partner. It also gives you a chance to take your clothes off yourself, instead of worrying about the quivering hands of someone who is desperately trying to remove your new fifty-dollar French dungarees, despite the fact that you still have your boots on. You must be careful, however, not to ruin the erotic mood by attempting something unsuitable and that might cause you to look foolish. Overweight women would do well to avoid body movements that require excessive swinging and swaying, or leaping. A *grand jeté* or a hula is not a good choice.

Belly dancing	100
Actually dancing with partner's belly	165

Note: Unless you are obsessively neat, wait until afterward to hang up your clothes and insert shoe trees.

Weight Loss Bonus #2

Activity	Calories burned
Stage fright	18

Can occur when both partners are finally naked and realize they will soon have to quit stalling and get on with it. Chief symptoms of stage fright are anxiety, nausea and an irrational need to either sleep or flee. It can usually be conquered by locking yourself in the bathroom and releasing the "bad energies" with a plunger.

Embarrassment

Calorie counts indicate amount of energy expended when coping with feelings of embarrassment and disgrace induced by:

Activity	Calories burned
Large juice stain on shorts	10
Holes in underwear	
If you are rich	2
If you are poor	20
Excessive hair in unusual places	
Pubic hair extends to feet	25
Hair around nipples (for man)	½
(for woman)	8
Cellulites	12
Large pores	10
Tattoo with raised lettering	18
Bloodshot nose	14
Bags over the eyes	66

Disappointment

Clothing can conceal and lie, causing many people to feel disappointed, even cheated, upon seeing their partner naked. In some cases, a less intimate activity may be preferred, such as watching a game show. A man who looks great in a suit turns out to have shoulders only eight inches wide, a chest like a raisin and legs like bleached sticks. A woman removes her shoes, shrinks from 5'7" to 4'9" and no one can find her. The following are some common disappointments and the calories burned in dealing with them:

Activity	Calories burned
Partner looked better with clothes on ....10 *(You may prefer sex with your partner's clothes.)*	
Partner looks better with your glasses off 10	
Partner's body resembles a tubercular chicken 12	
Partner wears corrective underwear 15	
Partner's sweater turns out to be hair on his/her chest 20	
Partner turns out to be of wrong sex ....100 You don't mind ....¼	
Partner turns out to be of wrong religion 57	
Partner wears elevated shoes 12	
Partner wears elevated socks 50	

Typical reactions to sexual disappointment

Setting bed on fire 8
Setting partner on fire 15
Suicide 1
Profound depression 9
Weeping:
    internal 27
    external 4
Laughter:
    controlled 5
    hysterical 14

Inventing complicated but believable excuse for leaving ("I have to go," is one example)..........5

Getting into Bed

Activity	Calories burned
Lifting partner	15
Straining	20
Turning red	5
Deciding who sleeps on the good side of the bed (the side closest to the kitchen)	14

No longer male-dominated activities. Many a woman, especially the strong, silent type, will take pride in lifting her partner, carrying him into the bedroom and gently tossing him onto the bed. Men appreciate this gesture, especially if they're tired and have to go to work, although there may be a few who feel threatened.

For those not strong enough for the above procedure, drag your partner along the floor	16
Using skateboard	3
Shivering from cold sheets	9
Shivering from fear	19
Setting snooze alarm	1
Placing teeth in glass of water	3
(applies only if they're false or very loose)	
Saying prayers	1
Tucking each other in	547

One couple got in and out of bed 137 times before realizing that it couldn't be done.

III. Foreplay

"You've got to start somewhere."
        DR. SHIRLEY EINSTEIN, NOTED THERAPIST

Professional dieters tell us that one burns more calories
during foreplay than during any other stage of sex, with
the possible exception of dancing in a tweed grope
suit or intercourse in the back-to-back position. It is
easy to see why. Foreplay is a time to experiment and try
new things—magic caresses with a kipper, love bites if
you have good teeth, bouncing with abandon and
ricocheting off the wall and arousing each other by making ridiculous faces.

   Those, on the other hand, who regard foreplay as
drudgery may prefer to skip directly to intercourse and
hope their partner won't notice.

Ten Alternate Erogenous Zones

(Should regular zones temporarily wear out)

1. Back of lips
2. Between the toes
3. Either bicuspid
4. Either vocal cord
5. Calluses
6. The taste buds
7. Any unpolished nail
8. The pinky ring
9. Any part of the endocrine system
10. Third shelf of the refrigerator

Being Good in Bed

Information here is for preparation only. Detailed descriptions and specific calorie counts are covered in the rest of the chapter.

The ideal male partner

- Willingly pitches in
- Lasts a long time before orgasm
- Is not distracted by fog, hiccups or reprimands
- Does quite well in at least six different positions
- Gives partner multiple orgasms
- Gives himself multiple orgasms
- Has a sense of timing which permits simultaneous orgasm
- Doesn't keep asking, "How am I doing?"
- Doesn't scold partner or grow sullen if she gets dressed and leaves
- Cheerfully gives post- and pre-coital back rubs
- Screams and yells only in bed
- Always removes his watch

Being Good in Bed

The ideal female partner

- Doesn't mind if partner gives her multiple orgasms
- Lasts only two minutes before first orgasm
- Doesn't wake the neighbors
- Enjoys being aggressive
- Doesn't feel used if partner collapses after four hours of sex
- Doesn't make a face during oral sex
- Lets partner do anything within reason
- Doesn't keep asking, "How are you doing?"
- Stays awake throughout
- Is attentive to partner after orgasm
- Can administer first aid
- Has plenty of food in the refrigerator
- Doesn't say "poor baby" if man has an orgasm while switching off the light

Being Even Better in Bed

Activity	Calories burned
Honestly telling partner what gets you excited	5

Going Too Far

Activity	Calories burned
Calming horrified partner	163

Writing

(An excellent muscle-loosener)

Activity	Calories burned
From	
Pleasure	12
Pain	12¼
Tickling	16
(Add five calories if partner is holding you down.)	
Cramps	9
Something you ate	20

Additional muscle looseners

Somersaults	15
Gross contortions	28

Teasing

When done in moderation, teasing your partner with a tongue (preferably yours) can be highly erotic and an effective calorie burner.

Activity	Calories burned
Licking partner all over but being careful to avoid all sexually sensitive areas ....20 *(With hairy partners, it will be necessary to periodically pause and dredge the mouth.)*	
Constantly resisting frustrated partner who is desperately trying to push your head toward sexually sensitive areas 35	

Note: Overdoing this procedure will cause your partner to become peevish and attempt to direct your tongue to sensitive areas by grasping and pulling on it, and not caring whether your head goes along.

Stroking

Activity	Calories burned
With	
Feather	4
Hand	6
Tips of fingers	7
Tips of toes	68
Frankfurter	15
Suede cat-o'-nine-tails	22
Fly swatter	14
Nervous dog	50
Magic Marker	11

Oral Sex

Activity	Calories burned
Cunnilingus	15
Nosebleed *(can be caused by over-excited partner)*	5
Fellatio *(Requires almost twice the effort of cunnilingus since it uses more muscles, especially those of the neck, hands and eyes.)*	30
Attempting to breathe through a severely stuffed nose	14
Hat trick	187
Toe sucking	12
With shoes on	49

One of the great advantages of oral sex is that if both partners are in fairly good health, it can go on almost indefinitely. The only adverse side effects will be a temporary lapse in the efficiency of the taste buds and difficulty in chewing anything harder than applesauce.

Removing Hair

Activity	Calories burned

From tongue 3
A relatively simple operation involving thumb
and index finger. Try to be discreet.

From roof of mouth 8
Slightly more complicated. Finger and tip
of tongue may be necessary.

From soft palate 14
Very complicated, especially if it is
sticking. You may have to use tongue plus a
couple of fingers, possibly even your whole
fist. If this doesn't work, try a fork.

From uvula 20
If hair is wrapped around uvula, it is easily
extractable with pliers or a vacuum
cleaner. Partner may notice.

From throat 23
Unless there's a small mop handy, you're
better off just swallowing the hair. Only
two calories per strand, no matter what the
color.

Disposing of Hair

Once you have successfully extracted the hair, you must dispose of it without offending your partner. ("Love me, love my hair.") Jettisoning it over the side of the bed would seem logical, except that a strand of hair is so light that it will probably stick to your fingers. You'll end up shaking your hand violently and accomplishing nothing except destroying the mood. Consider the following options:

Activity	Calories burned
Surreptitiously wiping it on sheet	1
Wiping it on partner *(A good idea, but the hair may come back to haunt you.)*	3
Putting it back where you found it *(The drilling motions may disturb your partner.)*	28

Note: We suggest hiding it underneath your arm until later.

Achieving Erection

Activity	Calories burned
For normal healthy man	2¼
For normal healthy woman	549
For man who is forty-six, folds his clothes neatly and still lives with his mother *(especially if she's waiting downstairs in a taxi)*	78

Sustaining Erection

Activity	Calories burned
For man	4
For woman	163

Some men consider this to be a woman's responsibility and just lie there, hoping that something will happen. For the woman this is good, since fighting gravity gives her the chance to burn lots of calories. One woman reports that she spent three hours trying to arouse a timid deacon, during which time she lost two pounds but grew so weak that her life began to flash before her eyes.

Weight Loss Bonus #3

Activity	Calories burned
Losing erection	¼
Searching for it	115

Putting on Prophylactic

Activity	Calories burned
With erection	1¼
Without erection	300

It is generally best to wait until you're ready, although some men try to save time by putting it on in advance—while still in the elevator or else during dinner. This seldom works.

Note: Myopic men should allow a minimum of ten extra calories and an additional five minutes.

Inserting Diaphragm

Activity	Calories burned

If woman who does it is

    Experienced 6

    Inexperienced.................................73

        If man does it regardless of experience 680

Add five calories for retrieving it from across the room—
add 100 if you leave it there.

Delays

Frigidity 11

Some common causes:

- Partner is wearing "Days of the Week" boxer shorts and garters
- Partner's foreplay technique consists of lighting a cigar and ordering food from Chicken Delight
- Partner refuses to show you his vasectomy scar
- Fear of feeling obligated
- Hunger pangs and you've just eaten
- Partner keeps asking, "Are you there yet?"
- Television too loud
- Television too soft
- Lack of privacy (maid keeps running in and asking for milk and cookies)
- Brim of partner's hat keeps hitting your forehead
- Large oil painting of Karl Marx on ceiling

Further Delays

Activity	Calories burned
Impotence	11

Some common causes:

- Desire to be trendy
- Subtle defense mechanism against giving or receiving v.d.
- Senility
- Harassment by a large dog
- Three-minute time limit
- Eight glasses of wine
- Fear of success
- Sixth attempt in an hour
- Hangover
- Partner's locket, when she's on top, keeps going in your mouth

Note: So long as neither partner gets upset, there is nothing to worry about and sex should proceed as if everything were normal.

Emotional Distress

Activity	Calories burned

Emotional Distress 22
    A mild breakdown—hysteria, withdrawal,
sitz baths, etc.—is a common and often
pleasant reaction to an attack of impotence
or frigidity.* If you are basically healthy,
however, there is little to worry about
unless your partner exhibits hostile
behavior by picking up the phone and
inviting someone better to come over.
You will then spend the next two months
wandering around in slippers and pajamas
and eating TV dinners without defrosting
them.

---

*Those who suffer from impotence *and* frigidity should see a doctor of some sort.

IV. Intercourse and Things Related

Intercourse usually follows directly after foreplay, except in the case of extremely spirited foreplay, in which case it might be wise to wait a day or two. Since intercourse puts such a severe strain on our physical and mental resources, we should be alert to the twelve warning signs of sexual enfeeblement:

---

1. Indifference to Renaissance architecture
2. Manic lips
3. A ringing in the mouth
4. Fingers won't snap
5. Palpitating liver
6. Loss of all sensation below hairline
7. A morbid craving for flanken
8. Vastly improved high notes
9. Change of blood type
10. Herniated salivary gland
11. Persistent need for juice
12. Motion sickness

Doing It for the First Time

Don't panic if the earth doesn't move. The first time around is usually more intellectual than physical. Many people, in fact, find themselves drawn to the word "fiasco" when called upon to describe their initial experience. "Catastrophe," "botch," "tragedy" and "lawsuit" are also sometimes used. Most problems, however, dissolve with time, patience and two or three hundred partners' worth of experience. Indeed, it is not unusual for the sexually gifted to go from hideous incompetence to blatant greatness within a four-year period. Following are some first time problems:

Activity	Calories burned
Fumbling around	4
Desperately trying to put something somewhere	18
Completely missing	9
Embarrassment	15
Disappointment (the famous "You mean that's it?" syndrome)	27
Scorn	30

Any traumatic episode
    Inadvertently, but expertly bringing pillow
    to orgasm
	60

Partner dozes off	41

Doing It for the Last Time

Following are the calories burned according to the most common reasons for swearing off intercourse.

Activity	Calories burned
New Year's resolution	15
Age	
Too old	1½
Too young	1¼
Something better happens along	5
Lack of time	11
Religious conversion	15
Discovering that intercourse detracts from foreplay	22
Bed repossessed	16

Doing It

Activity	Calories burned
Deciding position	
Tossing coin	2
Cutting cards	2½
Eenie meenie meiny murray	3
Attempting insertion	
Using hands	4
Using feet	500
While still deciding position	288

Insertion

Activity	Calories burned
If man is ready	¼
If woman is not	274

Insertion

Activity	Calories burned
If woman is ready	¼
If man is not	274

Satisfying Partner

(Organ size)

Most experts agree that size means nothing. Shape is what counts, and the man with an H-shaped organ can write his own ticket. In those rare instances where a man has a genuinely small member,* he may have to compensate by working slightly harder, but this is good for weight loss. A man with a really large organ,† while he might not have to work as hard once inside, may exhaust himself just trying to convince his partner to let him put it inside.

Activity	Calories burned
Normal size	22
Oversize	15
Tremendous	8
Teensy-weensy	163

*¼ to ½ inch
†2 feet and up

Positions

Constantly experimenting with new positions not only presents an opportunity to show off, but also lets you exercise the body, lose weight and rescue your sex life from monotony. Happily, the number of possible positions is nearly infinite, even more if you use a foot stool. The Royal Academy of Tibet recognizes over 860,* the Turkish Book of Delights lists 525 and the United Nations officially sanctions 203. It would be a rare couple indeed who couldn't find at least ten fully functional and highly satisfying ways to show each other that they care. Mentioned below are but a few of the more popular positions, all of which combine maximum weight loss with productive body contact. Select those that work best for you and don't be discouraged if it takes a little time to get them perfect.

Activity	Calories burned
Man on top, woman on bottom (facing each other)....20	
Man on top, woman on bottom (back to back).......749	

Woman on top, man on bottom 25
    Many women find that in addition to its
    inherent sexual possibilities, this position
    affords a better view of the clock.	

*804 are quite useless, however, unless you already are a helpless cripple and have nothing left to lose.

Standing
Both partners of equal height 18
Woman one foot taller than man 90
(The man will have to make several rigorous leaps into the air in order to achieve even minimal satisfaction.)

While in traction...................................124
(very useful during ski season)

Immelmann roll 67
A slight variation on the so-called
reverse missionary position; the
adventuresome will find it amusing. While
on top, the woman raises her left thigh and
places it behind her neck, all the while
rotating her pelvis until she is spinning out
of control, thus inducing her partner to feel
useful. Not only is this position visually
agreeable, but it permits the woman to
reach an impressive climax without
actually snapping her spine. (Not
recommended for those convalescing.)

From the rear (mysterious variation) 40½
Accomplished with the man on his
knees, thighs spread, his elbows resting on
a pillow, his head against the wall. The
woman then approaches from the rear and
wonders what to do.

Positions According to Nationality

Italian: man on top, woman in kitchen 26

English: woman on top, man in hiding 15

German: facing each other but in different beds 48

Oriental: man in front, woman three paces behind ...51

Russian: woman on bottom, man getting permission ..55

American: both on top 60

Locations

(Additional calorie counts for places other than bed.)

Activity	Calories burned
In suburbia	3½
On a bar stool	20
Rear of a Honda Civic	38

In a phone booth
Standing	14
Lying down	274

Activity	Calories burned
On a lawn chair (plastic webbing)	88
Under a pyramid	?

On an airliner
Aisle seat	24
Middle seat (fat passenger on either side)	42
Window seat	30
In the lavatory	100

In a hammock (on a breezy day) 50
Add 25 calories if only one end is tied to tree.

In a van with bad springs 11

It should also be noted that pleasure is heightened when sex takes place spontaneously—during a movie, during Lent, while backing out of the driveway, etc.

Intercourse

Activity	Calories burned
Starting (overcoming inertia)	¼
Moderate (sort of gliding along)	15
Heavy (enthusiastically involved)	27
Merciless pounding	50
Incoherent convulsions	75
Shock	100
Blacking out	125
Hernia	150
Heart attack	227
Death	1

Possible Side Effects of Intercourse

Activity	Calories burned
Bouncing	7
Sliding around	9
Serious skidding	12
Full cartwheel	20
Whiplash	27
Knee burn	6
Chafed elbows	5
Chafed nose	11

Sex-Related Noises

Activity	Calories burned
Giggling	7
Laughing	11
Short gasps (per gasp)	3
Wheezing	5
Squeals	4
Ecstatic moaning	11
Low growling	8
Squishing	10
Shouting	16
Screaming	18
Urgent begging	22
Any short speech giving partner directions *("Please don't stop," "Just a little more," "Faster," "one inch more and make a sharp right" are common examples)*	25

If it embarrasses you that your neighbors might hear, merely stuff partner's mouth with any citrus fruit.

Seeking Comfort

Activity	Calories burned
Switching positions 16	
Without stopping 41	

Unless you have nonskid sheets, the slipping and sliding caused by sexual activity may result in a good deal of lateral movement, and you may end up in some extraordinarily uncomfortable and totally unworkable positions.*

Changing positions is advised should any of the following occur:

- You find yourself teetering at the edge of the bed and a vicious dog with paws akimbo is waiting for you to fall.
- One of you actually falls off the bed. (If you continue to have intercourse, add one hundred calories.)
- You suddenly discover that one of your shoulders is on the bed and the other is touching the floor.
- You've moved up too far and your head is repeatedly slamming into the wall in time to the thrusts, making it difficult to concentrate and keep your tiara on.
- One leg has become so entangled in the sheets that the foot is turning green and gangrene appears imminent.
- A stupendous thrust blasts you both through the window, thereby putting all chances of a really satisfying orgasm in jeopardy.

*In extreme cases, couples can cover as many as four miles during three hours of really intensive sex. One couple, after starting out in the bedroom, found themselves, two hours later, dodging bowling balls in the third lane of Archie's Bowl-O-Rama on League Night. They were upset.

Approaching Orgasm

Activity	Calories burned
Letting go	5½
Controlling yourself	79
Digging nails into back	
Your partner's	11
Your own	165
Shifting gum	1
Chewing faster	2
Much faster	3½
Trembling	15
Shaking	20
Shuddering	25
Trying to keep eyes open	33

Orgasm

Activity	Calories burned
Real	27
Faked	160

Orgasmic Intensity Scale

Activity	Calories burned
Shoes flew off	35
Expression didn't change	½
Room turned purple	4
Face turned purple	15
Orchestra swelled	6
Birds sang	
Large birds	7
Small birds	3
Magical explosions	10
Trumpets blared	12
Flutes blared	2
Roman candles	14
Blazing pinwheels	16
Blazing sheets	25
Earth moved	30
Vesuvius erupted	47
You began moaning in Latin	60

Pulling Out

(Un-insertion)

Activity	Calories burned
After orgasm	¼
A few moments before orgasm	500

Multiple Orgasms for Female

Activity	Calories burned
Two	14
Five	30
Eight	47
Fifteen	106

Depending on greed—and her rate of recovery—a woman can enjoy up to eight orgasms within a one-hour period without losing consciousness or disarranging her hair. As the number increases, however, she may begin to experience a form of "reduced sanity" that will temporarily interfere with her ability to cook, worship and ride a Moped.

Multiple Orgasms for Male

Activity	Calories burned
Two	21
Three	39
Four	57
Twelve	?*

For a man, it's a different situation, perhaps due to physiological and biological reasons. Many men can enjoy up to four orgasms in an hour with little discomfort except for a slight ringing in the ears. With few exceptions, however, a man who tries to achieve more than ten orgasms within that same period is flirting with irreversible brain damage.

*Subject lapsed into a coma too soon afterward to tell.

Special Orgasms

Activity	Calories burned
Clitoral	15
Vaginal	21
Penile	21
Scrotile	15
Rectal	25
Oral *(can also occur during an especially good meal)*	30
Futile	1

Premature Ejaculation*

(For male)

Activity	Calories burned
During insertion	2
During intercourse *(approximately two seconds or three thrusts after insertion, whichever comes first)*	5
During foreplay *(while scrambling eggs, for example)*	3
During dinner (very premature)	1
While parking the car (over-anticipation)	¼
Immature ejaculation *(similar to premature ejaculation except male acts childish and throws a tantrum)*	4

*Often caused by an inability to do things right.

Consequences of Premature Ejaculation for Female

Even if you have a good heart, it takes much understanding not to feel like a victim when your partner climaxes after three seconds of intensive sex, especially if he immediately sits up to watch the Rose Bowl game.

Activity	Calories burned
Frustration	8
Anger	15
Violent mood swing	20
Suppressing rage	25
Not suppressing rage In extreme cases, this can include cursing, nose tweaks, and gently massaging partner's head with a tire iron.	65

Note how unfair: Men never seem to mind if a woman has an orgasm after three seconds of sex.

Consequences of Premature Ejaculation for Male

Activity	Calories burned
Cursing	10
Apologizing	3
Sniveling	5
Pleading for mercy	8
Begging for another chance	15

Achieving Orgasm Under Unusual Circumstances

Activity	Calories burned
While donating blood	45
After two bottles of wine *(Even insertion may be a problem.)*	50
While talking on the telephone	15
On a mushy bed	11
With close relatives in the room	60
While negotiating for a loan	100
During a job interview	100
During intercourse	8

Delaying Orgasm

Medical evidence suggests that prolonged procrastination of orgasm (four to six weeks) impedes the flow of vital juices, making you feel bloated and not at peace with the world. Delaying orgasm for a reasonable time, however, causes little harm and may be necessary in order to accommodate a slow partner. A man whose partner has been repeating the phrase, "not yet," over a two-hour period will find it necessary to hold off. At a certain point, though, he will become desperate and wonder if he's going to die. Women, occasionally, find it convenient to postpone orgasm if they think they're going to hate themselves in the morning or, at the very latest, right after lunch. Following are some tips on how to delay orgasm without leaving the room:

- Think about your teeth.
- Rethink the Mideast crisis.
- Take a pencil and total a recent supermarket receipt either on the pillowcase or your partner's forehead.

V. Afterward

What happens directly after sex can be just as important as what happened during. Some people immediately light a cigarette. Others immediately put theirs out. Generally, however, most people concentrate on making their partner feel that it was totally satisfying and wonderful. This is easily accomplished by just lying there and looking contented (a vapid stare is good), instead of rushing into the bathroom and scrubbing yourself with Ajax.

Weight Loss Bonus #4

Activity	Calories burned
Avoiding the wet spot	20

Things Often Said After Sex

Activity	Calories burned
All Post-Coital Utterances	15

Examples:

"Continue Sedation!"
"Your wig is on backward."
"Was it good for you?"
"I'm so grateful."
"It must have been something we ate."
"Don't do that again."
"How's it going?" (also said during intercourse)
"I've got such a headache."
"Get out."
"Congratulations."
"Are you finished?"
"Am I finished?"
"It's a miracle."
"You did it wrong."
"I'm exhausted."
"Please help me."
"When do we eat?"

Possible Side Effects of Good Sex

The first indication that sex was a positive experience will be a buzzing in the pelvic area and a clear complexion. You might also feel pleasantly light, as though you were dozing in a vat of cream cheese. If sex was really terrific, you feel dangerously drained, as though your body had been connected to a large milking machine for several days. Additional reactions include:

Activity	Calories burned
Swooning	6
Palpitations	10
Shortness of breath	5
Perspiring	8
Amnesia	22
Bronchitis	25
Mild gum damage	12

Possible Side Effect of Bad Sex

Activity	Calories burned
A less-than-sunny disposition 1	

Recovering

Activity	Calories burned
Un-entwining	3

Regaining motor control of pelvis 7
    After especially tiring sex, you may
    feel numb from below the waist to the
    opposite wall. The result will be an
    inability to walk (put one foot in front of the
    other), which will seriously impair your
    chances of going to the bathroom or getting
    food.

Standing up 9

Getting some juice 11

Expressing thanks 2

Rolling Over and Going to Sleep

Activity	Calories burned
Activity	**Calories burned**

After intercourse 18
> Classic behavior for shiftless men who believe they've done their job and are now entitled to a rest. This "rest" may include snoring.

During intercourse 32
> Women find this to be a subtle, yet direct way of suggesting dissatisfaction.

During foreplay 12
> Indicates either an advanced case of fatigue or a serious lack of interest.

While still in the kitchen 5
> Situation hopeless.

Rolling over and falling off the bed 2

Sleep

Activity	Calories burned
Real	5

Faked	74

A good way to avoid a sex-crazed partner who simply won't give up. Faking sleep is also a reliable escape technique when, after sex, you suddenly find yourself wishing that you could make your partner disappear. This may happen when you go to bed with somebody just for sex, which is a sin.

Trying Again

Activity	Calories burned
If woman is ready	5
If man is not	156

Tidying and Cleaning Up

Activity	Calories burned
Racing partner to bathroom	
Barefoot	6
In floppy slippers	18
In sloppy flippers	50

Showering

Activity	Calories burned
Alone	7

(To burn extra calories, hold the soap perfectly still and move your body.)

With partner	12

With a waterpik	133

With no hot water	187

(includes writhing and making hideous faces)

Taking a bath together
    In the tub 5
    In the sink 28

Damp mopping each other 10

Brushing each other's teeth 25

Drying Off

Activity	Calories burned

Using
    Luxurious bath towel 6
    Large hand towel...............................9
    Small washcloth 15
    Two squares of toilet tissue 21

In front of fan 1

Spinning and hopping 37

Making the Bed

Activity	Calories burned
With partner still in it	44

(Indicates either a neatness obsession, a severe optic disorder or a partner who is very tired.)

With you still in it	97

(Suggests extreme withdrawal and profound dissatisfaction.)

Mending furniture	22
Rinsing sheets	25
Just shaking them out	15
Removing candle wax	10

VI. Supplementary Activities

So much activity is compressed into sex that we sometimes fail to realize that weight loss is going on constantly, and sometimes when we least expect it. Did you know, for instance, that fantasizing can burn an additional twenty calories, even more if you despair? Or that a depraved bondage-and-scolding session may actually reduce your waistline? In this section we will see how the so-called fringe areas of sex can play an important role not only in caloric consumption, but in making sex something special.

Male Fantasies

Fantasy can be used for anything from enhancing an already terrific sexual experience to blocking out a dull partner and concentrating on something more pleasant. Surviving eight minutes with a trucker named Earl who talked you into bed over his CB radio, for example, might be accomplished by fantasizing about sex with a polished Nazi who sings Wagner in your ear. Following are some common sexual fantasies and the calories burned while thinking about them.

Activity	Calories burned
Sex slave to five insomniac starlets	18
Sex with a Quaker named Natasha	14
Casual intercourse with a warm bugle	9
Foreplay with a skittish frog	11
"Love wrestling" with an elk	22
Sex with a chicken wearing a tiny rubber raincoat	15
Making love to bread	5
Sex in a knapsack (constrictus claustrophobus)	12

Female Fantasies

Activity	Calories burned
Wild intercourse with a jolly butcher	20
Foreplay with a hallucinating accountant	17
Doing it in downtown Sheboygan	40
Getting ravished by a senator	9
An afternoon in bed with a caring dolphin	15
Sex with a Latin dance instructor who wears taps on his feet	23
Being dragged into a burning building by a cowardly dog named Herman	12
Sex with a virile renegade	25

Dreaming

Activity	Calories burned
Regular dream	2
Wet dream	16
(Add five calories if it occurs while in bed with your partner; add twenty calories if your partner notices.)	
Dry dream	1
Wet trance	20
(Usually occurs in the presence of a sensual hypnotist.)	

Group Sex

Activity	Calories burned
Introducing yourself	3
Overcoming shyness	8
Swapping partners	
Willingly	4
Unwillingly	62
Jealousy (partner having more fun than you are)	16
Mixed doubles	26
Being nice to everyone	100
Identity crisis	18
Anger	10

(You suddenly realize that you're wanted for your body and not your mind. Difficult to cope with, especially if you have a Ph.D.)

Finding your clothes	5

Masturbation

Activity	Calories burned
For pleasure only	6
For exercise, too	10
For relief from tension	12
To pass the time	7
To avoid overeating	16
To get in touch with inner self	10
To get in touch with outer self	10¼
To avoid insanity	24
To avoid spending money on a date	9

In addition to being a viable alternative to television, shopping and binges, masturbation is a quick and inexpensive way to get warm.

Using

Your hand(s): regular way 11

behind the back 500

your finger(s) 9

Tweezers 2

An inflatable doll named Heidi 24

A hand mike 14

Tight dungarees 17

Any fruit or vegetable (except watermelon
or a sprig of parsley) 19

A sandwich (no mayo, hold the lettuce) 15

A shower massage 5

A vibrator:

hand-operated................................12

windup.......................................9

electric 5

diesel (still in testing stages) 74

Anything not mentioned above 50

In a pornographic movie theater:

Purchasing ticket...........................2½

Finding isolated seat before eyes adjust to
darkness 78

Tripping and stumbling........................50

Adjusting raincoat 3

Fetishism

There is nothing abnormal about complementing one's sexual activities with objects generally found in a less erotic setting. Certain people, for example, achieve total gratification only when wearing linoleum shoes. Others prefer foreplay with sailors who wax their legs. An erotic devotion to items such as leather, copper, dough and stockings merely suggests that you think for yourself instead of following others. For additional weight loss, try one of the popular fetishes below:

Activity	Calories burned
Sex with a partner wearing armor	472
Sex while wearing a rubber watch	9
Sex on a three-inch merry-go-round	146
Any kipper fetish	23
Insisting partner wear a plastic yarmulke with earflaps	17
Sex in a frog outfit	58
Sex with a partner wearing leather body boots	97

Bondage

Along with enhancing the sexual experience, bondage will also prevent a gluttonous partner from eating all the food. A reliable bondage device can be anything from a nylon stocking or a length of industrial chain to an ultrasophisticated restraint system such as a roll of adhesive tape and suspenders.

Activity   **Calories burned**

Binding partner with rope (the following knots are favorites):

Sheepshank	7
Slipknot	8
Half hitch	9
Figure eight	11
Square knot	12

Binding partner with a necktie

Windsor knot	9
Half Windsor	4½

For the awkward, we suggest

Handcuffs	3
Shackles	6
Leg irons	5
Glue	10

Escapage

Struggling to get free while partner is tickling your feet	41
Untying knots	
Using fingernails	7
Without using fingernails	22

Discipline

An excellent high-calorie activity, especially if your partner objects.

Activity	Calories burned

Thrashing partner with
    Popsicle stick 2
    Shoelace 2
        (add another ten calories if still in shoe)
    Chopstick 4
    Tongue depressor 4
    Chicken wing 6
        (add twelve calories if still attached to chicken)
    Oar 15
    Drive shaft of a luxury car 20

Whipping

(Making Whippie)

Activity	Calories burned
Using high-quality whip (per stroke) 3	
Includes handle made of Italian leather wrapped around ebony, good balance and a built-in AM/FM radio. Gucci makes a very stylish initialed lash.	
Using cat-o'-nine-tails 27	
Flogging a moving hen 10	

Weight Loss Bonus #5

Activity	Calories burned
Spanking (per spank) 5	

The most simple and satisfying form of spanking is laying your partner across your knees and then smacking the buttocks with an open hand. (In order to avert tragedy, make sure that your partner is lying face down.) Should your hand grow tired, feel free to use your partner's. For a significant increase in calories burned, slightly alter the above procedure by holding partner across your knees while you remain standing.

For those too exhausted for whipping, spanking, beating and similar manual tasks, but who still wish to enjoy some sort of discipline, we suggest relaxing in bed and just ordering your partner around. This requires little effort and saves much wear and tear on skin and bones.

Giving partner any of the following orders 3

> "Attention!"
> "Bring me a cookie, slave!"
> "Bite the carpet!"
> "Polish my feet!"
> "Hop around the room, on your hands!"

As a substitute for any of the above, you can scold your partner for imagined infractions.

Note: If partner is also tired, he or she can pretend to obey your orders by answering, "Right-o," without actually moving a muscle.

Sex with Animals

Activity	Calories burned
A grateful sheep	22
An irate warthog	150
A love-starved donkey	100
An eagle in flight	583
A virile field mouse	¼
A shy chicken	2
Any fish less than fourteen inches long	3
A graceful moose	79

Those who can't take criticism occasionally turn to the animal kingdom in their time of need, since the prospect of being scolded or having to make idle conversation is virtually nil.* The only drawbacks are a lack of meaningful communication and, in the case of larger animals such as lions, the danger of being eaten. Additionally, a noted sex therapist, in her book *Night at the Zoo,* maintains that forcing an animal to have sex against its will can have severe psychological repercussions, for the animal.

*You may occasionally have to say "Whoa!" or "Here, boy!"

Bizarre Sex Practices

Activity	Calories burned
Having partner jump on your face	70
Holding false teeth in hand and giving partner love bites	18
Foreplay while scuba diving	100
Sex on a vibrating bed	46

Sex on a vibrating bed 46
   Vibrating beds are usually found in
   motels frequented by people with back
   trouble. Look for a motel with a sign
   saying, "Welcome People with Back
   Trouble." These beds are activated either
   by dropping a coin in the slot or, if
   you're cheap, jumping the wires. Avoid
   vibrating beds if you've just eaten a lot of
   chili.

Gay Sex

Activity	Calories burned
Jolly foreplay	4
Light-hearted impotence	1
Jaunty erection	3
Hilarious coitus	6
Reckless positions	6
Lively moaning	2
Shouting with joy	3
Madcap orgasm	7
Jocular ejaculation	5
Post-orgasmic rejoicing	6
Genial fatigue	2
Convulsing partner with a joke	3
Rolling on floor with laughter	4
Rolling on partner with laughter	6
Good-natured sadism	8
Buoyant bondage	7
Dancing on the bed	10

Additional Erotic Experiences

(For "quickie" weight loss)

Activity	Calories burned
Watch partner shave	4
Drink from a Jacuzzi	10
Eat a 1-pound square of fudge, with tweezers	40
Study an Irish cookbook	1
Smoke an unfiltered herring	13
Roll around nude in a bakery window	72
Wink each other off	90
Close a business deal	50
Caress your stereo system	30
Lick a Porsche all over	100
Cook a fifteen-course dinner together without using any utensils	80
Have sex on vinyl sheets	18
Hold a Tupperware party	82
Tape-record your love cries and play them for your dentist	51

Keeping a Journal

In addition to this book, maintaining your own record of sexual activity will be helpful for keeping track of weight loss. You needn't go into great detail; just list the activity and the number of calories burned. A typical entry in a woman's journal—for example—for a pleasant, low-key sexual experience might read as follows:

June 1: Sex with Harold

Activity	Calories burned
Explaining how	12
Suggesting something different	3
Calming terrified Harold	40
Encouraging him to at least take off his socks	8
Foreplay (a little of this, a little of that)	56
Intercourse	
Standing position	22
Holding Harold up	10
Urging him on	5
Orgasm	not sure
Thanking Harold	3
Waving bye-bye	1

Total time: six minutes (taxi waiting)

Total Calories Burned [160]

VII. Miscellaneous Problems, Emergencies And Disasters

"Most serious accidents occur within 50 miles of home."

CHAUNCEY FARNUM, C.L.U.

The following pages list the calories burned when coping with stress situations often encountered during sex, including shock, anxiety, fear, annoyance and discomfort. All are easily survivable if you have a sense of humor, or can get dressed quickly.

*There are exceptions. A Persian tourist fell off her bike in Los Angeles and a fat American tore his pants while positioning himself on a barstool in Ezio's Clam Bar, Rome, Italy.

Penis Envy

Activity	Calories burned
For woman	3
For man	72

Typical Sex-Related Fears

(Rational and irrational)

Activity	Calories burned
Partner hates me for what I did	4
Partner hates me for what I didn't do	8
At any moment my grandparents will enter the room and quietly sit down	5
Forgetting the instructions in the sex manual	10
Climaxing too soon	5
Climaxing too late	6
Not climaxing	20
Partner thinks of me as a sex object	9
Partner doesn't think of me as a sex object	47
Partner will neglect to administer last rites should I not recover from orgasm	88

Personal Fears

Some shortcomings, real and imagined, that your partner might be noticing:

Activity	Calories burned
Breath smells like a wino's hat	4
Gigantic cellulites that shake and ripple during orgasm	6
Stretchmarks that look like a plowed field	8
Large pores	5
No pores	10
Poorly capped teeth that wiggle	11
Excessive hair under arms	3
A roll of fat around the middle that becomes especially prominent when you sit down	20
Body odor of a disgruntled yak	25

Note: It has been pointed out that people who were toilet trained late (teens to early twenties) have a remarkable fear of everything.

Guilt

(Frequently used by masochists to compensate for happiness.)

Activity	Calories burned

From

     Masturbation 10

     Liking sex 7

     Loving sex 20

     Never wanting to stop except to take your
temperature...................................30

Possible guilt situations

Despite almost no formal training, orgasm
     comes easily, naturally and spontaneously 53

You're enjoying sex, despite the fact that
     other people are starving 2

Sex on your lunch hour 3

And you put it on your expense report 20

Aggravation

Although science has yet to determine precisely why aggravation burns calories, we do know that people, when aggravated, lose weight—possibly because they stamp their feet. Below are several typical situations encountered during sex.

Activity	Calories burned
Partner keeps showing you his/her plants	5
Partner insists on cuddling dog during foreplay	14
Partner just visited bathroom for seventh time	10
Partner is taking phone calls	7
Partner is making phone calls	40
Partner refuses to remove jewelry, including watch, stickpin, I.D. bracelet, locket and flea collar	20

More Aggravation

Activity	Calories burned
Rejection	24

It is a sign of rejection if partner:

- Insists that you keep your feet out the window
- Brings a bottle of champagne with a screw-off cap
- Attempts shock therapy with a toaster
- Attempts to rob you
- Tries to make the bed during foreplay
- Serves warm 7-Up
- Asks you to take down the garbage
- Sharpens a knife on the side of your head
- Doesn't remove gloves
- Tries to fold your fingers the wrong way
- Keeps sending telegrams
- Puts a bear trap on the pillow

Acquiring Bedsores

Activity	Calories burned
In bed	20
On a cheap carpet	5
On any surface generally used for industrial purposes	½

The danger of contracting bedsores from prolonged sexual activity is not remote, especially since bedsores are highly contagious. Indeed, couples have been known to emerge from bed, each of them covered by a large and hideous wound that extended from the nape of the neck to the Achilles tendon. To avoid this, partners are urged to de-bed at least once every hour, place sheets in the freezer, and perform at least ten minutes of exercises such as stretching, push-ups, sit-ups and backflips.

Note: Bedsores can also be avoided by generous application of Turtle Wax, olive oil or Pledge. In the case of especially severe bedsores, a slice of pizza has been known to make an effective poultice.

Getting Caught

Activity	Calories burned
By partner's spouse	60
By your spouse	60½
Trying to explain	165
Stuttering	28
Throwing up	40

Calorie counts here are flexible, depending on type of spouse—whether understanding and open-minded, or narrow-minded and armed.

Almost Getting Caught

Activity	Calories burned
Trying to remain calm	100
Fright (includes trembling)	66
Leaping out of bed	25
Getting dressed in one large motion	300
Thanking partner quickly	2
Jumping out of window *(Add five calories if window wasn't open.)*	15
Landing	1
Running very fast	50

Threatening Situations

Activity	Calories burned
Partner arrives wearing a leather leisure suit and sipping from a can of motor oil	34
Partner has brought a relative	40
Partner's slave fetish is getting out of hand	50
A surreptitious three-hour search fails to turn up partner's alleged vasectomy scar	100

Interruptions and Distractions

Activity	Calories burned
Somebody going peek-a-boo	15
Noisy neighbors	7
Skipping record	5
Excessive moonlight	¼
Skipping child	10
Partner wearing a silly hat	6
Telephone	4
Flock of geese	11
War	70
Bed catches fire	15
Hunger	9
Good Humor man ringing bells	14
Knock on door (Jehovah's Witness selling "The Watchtower").	10
Resuming where you left off	30

Afflictions

Activity	Calories burned

Leg Cramp 36

> A common affliction that strikes
> without warning. It generally afflicts those
> who attempt a position that conflicts with
> the laws of gravity or who have not warmed
> up sufficiently (see Chapter I). The result is
> a pressing need to straighten out the leg
> immediately, even if it means kicking your
> partner, falling on the floor and turning
> orgasm into a terrifying experience.

Sneezing
    During intercourse 7
    During oral sex
        For sneezer 19
        For sneezee 280

Note: Hay fever sufferers would do well to avoid having
      sex in a field of ragweed or in dusty bookshops.

Call of Nature

Activity	Calories burned
Going and getting it over with	8
Gritting teeth and holding out until you can't stand the pain	100

Nothing is more miserable than leaving a nice warm bed containing another nice warm body just to perform a chore. On the other hand, remaining in bed and hoping it will somehow go away never works, no matter how hard you pray.

Note: If your partner agrees, you can keep a porcelain potty under the bed for emergencies.

Fighting off Pets

Activity	Calories burned
Tiny nervous dogs weighing less than eight ounces	3
Playful Saint Bernard	20
Jealous Doberman	92
Any enraged mongrel	50
Cat	6
Resentful parakeet	2½

Although a determined sweep of the hand will usually work, we advocate a pistol, club or terrifically loud voice.

Assorted Accidents

Activity	Calories burned
Toupee slips off	
If partner knew you were wearing one	6
If partner didn't know	72
Passionate moaning causes dentures to fall out	28
Extinguishing cigarette	
In ashtray	1
In mattress	17
In partner's leg	133
Calling partner by wrong name	50
Bed collapses	10
Shorts explode during foreplay	90

VIII. Eating and Sex

(The Bedside Eater)

"Sex to nourish the soul, food to nourish the sex."
KARL "CARL" SCHUSSELDORF, NUTRITIONIST

Advanced thinkers have long been aware that the nutritional requirements of sex are, to say the least, awesome. Not only does intense sexual activity deprive the body of height and weight, but it also causes a rapid depletion of proteins, carbohydrates, riboflavin, oxygen, cereal fillers and vital minerals such as copper, zinc and aluminum. If these essential elements are not replaced soon, rigor mortis sets in and we begin to grow irritable. We must therefore recognize the importance of taking nourishment during any period of sexual activity exceeding fifteen minutes, lest we do irreversible damage to organs, glands and bone marrow.

We must not, however, undo the good work done thus far by stuffing ourselves with high caloric and fattening foods such as halvah, creamed spinach, Necco Wafers, jujubes and bean soup. Nor should we go to the other extreme; rigid dieting invites misery, and puritans who consider a cup of tea and polyunsaturated bean sprouts nutritionally sound generally suffer a premature death. There is no harm in relaxing our dietary vigil providing we do so with intelligence, seeking a happy medium between utter starvation and sheer piggery.

Best for bedside eating are foods that enhance the sexual experience—high energy aphrodisiacs containing the minimum adult daily requirement of satisfaction and yielding a high rate of pleasure per calorie: chocolate cake, ice cream (most flavors), caviar, chili con carne, pizza, spareribs and authentic ethnic foods such as Chinese, Italian, French and American. This, as opposed to foods yielding a vile rate of satisfaction per calorie: okra, crackers, parsley, watercress, Spam and codfish cakes. Mention should also be made of the fraudulent aphrodisiacs: Spanish fly, oysters, baby food, wheat germ, chicken pot pie, prunes and porridge, all of which are useless. And, finally, we counsel against what are capriciously known as "health" foods, most of which contribute to acute famishment, pellagra and depression.

The following refreshments were chosen by a panel of experts as those most often partaken of before, during, after—and way after—sex. These foods and beverages are held in high esteem not only for their nutritional value, but for their good taste and salubrious effect upon the psyche. If you happen to keep a small refrigerator beside the bed, so much the better. It will make the job of taking nourishment that much more convenient. As always, we recommend prudent indulgence, and never have sex directly after a heavy meal.*

---

*A heavy meal: truffled sausages, pâté, clam chowder (two bowls), meat loaf and french fries with green ravioli al Forno, assorted goat cheeses, four fudge brownies, beer, wine and Perrier. Dessert: a one-inch pizza (unsweeted) with everything on it.

Calories in Food

(Calorie counts listed below will vary according to ingredients, size of portion and dimensions of mouth.)

Food	Calories

Ice cream
> Per spoonful 14
> Per ladleful 84

> "Plasma for the soul," is how one eating specialist expressed her reverence for ice cream as she slowly demolished her second pint of rum raisin. Since the Renaissance, ice cream has been worshiped for its healing powers and ability to effect miraculous recoveries in people suffering from backache, tonsillitis, impotence, enlarged sweet tooth and other major disorders. In order to savor its fullest essence, ice cream should be eaten or sipped directly from the container, instead of placing it in a dish and risking contamination. This is especially important with flavors such as butter almond and pistachio, where too much handling may bruise the nuts. Many ice cream fetishists, in order to prevent melting and "flavor leakage" between store and home, transport their purchase in a refrigerated hat.

Creamsicle (per lick) 3
> A highly portable, easy-to-eat item that is suitable should you want some ice cream during intercourse. Be careful that it doesn't melt and drip into your partner's eye. After finishing use the stick for discipline (see Chapter VI).

Frozen custard (Dairy Queen, Carvel, etc.)

Per lick 3¼

Will do in a crisis, although it will probably
melt all over your wrist. If you have the
time, and need the exercise, go over to the
dispenser, affix your mouth directly to the
nozzle and ingest a pint or two without
bothering with a cone.

Pizza (per bite) 15

Builds strong bones and teeth. If you order
your pizza with extra cheese, meatballs,
anchovies, mushrooms and pepperoni
(known as the "Breath-burner Surprise"),
add a few calories. Although pizza is just a
bit clumsy to eat in bed, especially if it's
hot and you insert the entire slice into your
mouth at once, it is an excellent source of
potassium and vitamin D. Always order
pizza well in advance and have your money
ready. Fumbling for correct change while
the delivery person waits in the hall and
your partner waits in bed can make you feel
foolish.*

Leftover spaghetti (per strand) 3

This, too, is somewhat difficult to eat in
bed, but the nutritional benefits are well
worth it. Like good wine, a well-aged
spaghetti (sixteen to eighteen hours) can
make a glorious addition to bedroom
cuisine, a delicate yet substantial repast
that helps the body maintain its vim and
vigor, no matter what. If you've added
meatballs, so much the better. You can
throw them at each other should you grow
bored.

*In certain counties, a pizza delivery is considered to be a valid medical
emergency and delivery trucks are equipped with sirens.

Cold meat loaf (per handful) 14
  A stick-to-the-bedsheets dish that provides
  the necessary stamina for long-distance
  sex. Meat loaf is generally served with
  french fries, but in this case, we prefer
  something a bit lighter, like kasha.
  Weight-watchers take note: Cold meat loaf
  contains 1 percent fewer calories than
  warm meat loaf.

Brownie or fudge (per hearty nibble)................28
  Like ice cream, the restorative powers of
  brownies and fudge make them an
  indispensable part of bedroom eating.
  Indeed, one huge brownie, with a coating of
  perfect fudge (an "oxygen" brownie) pulled
  one couple out of a trance brought on by two
  days of steady sex, during which time they
  stopped only once to change the bed.

Cherries (per cherry, no stem) 2½
  One of the most refreshing of fruits,
  especially when served cold. Keep a spare
  cherry in your navel for emergencies and
  decoration. It will please your partner.
  Note: Cherries, which are rich in vitamin
  C, will help prevent scurvy.

Caviar:
  Per ounce 91
  Per egg 00.00047

  Erotically exotic and exotically erotic.
  Don't waste caviar on a second-rate
  partner. Wait until after you've had sex. If
  your partner wasn't any good, serve Cheese
  Doodles, instead. Caviar should be washed
  down with either champagne or a suitable
  substitute such as Dr. Brown's Cel-Ray
  tonic.

Snickers bar (per bite) 20
>Because of its sublime chewability, Snickers is considered to be a supreme example of dental satisfaction and the perfect flesh substitute, should you become tired of biting into your partner. It is one of the few candy bars that will accept a hickey.

Pâté (per smear) 22
>One of the most life-giving and sensuous of spreads is a country pâté comprised of veal, pork, brandy and garlic. It can be eaten directly from the knife, or, if you don't mind a few extra calories, smeared on bread. To revive those in the final stages of starvation, a renowned eating tutor suggests digging a trench in a two-foot loaf of French bread, packing it with pâté and, as he so eloquently puts it, "Stuffing your face until you faint."

Bread (per one-pound loaf) 1115.3
>If you are finicky, you may wish to cut the loaf into what dainty eaters call "slices," and then figure your calories accordingly. Healthy eaters, however, know the value of a good dose of bread and generally prefer to cut the loaf in half, hollow out the inside and fill it with peanut butter, eggplant or tuna fish.

Cheese (per hunk) 30
>For quick energy and performing nibbling exercises, a plate of assorted cheeses, all served at room temperature, should be a fundamental part of the bedroom repast. Sharp Cheddar, Jarlsberg, Brie, Edam, Gruyere, Taleggio, Pecorino and Roquefort are most recommended.

Hershey Kisses (per kiss) 21
      No matter how tired or hungry you are, do not
      neglect to remove the tinfoil or you'll be sorry,
      especially if you are in the midst of root canal
      work. Besides tasting good, Hershey Kisses are
      excellent for raising the blood sugar to an
      acceptable level. Hypoglycemiacs take note.

Chocolate cake (per bite)..........................26
      One of the few reliable cures for sexual
      dysfunction. In fact, the therapeutic effect
      of chocolate cake is such that people have
      been known to eat large slices of it even
      when they're not having sex.

Chili con carne (per spoonful) 10
      Vital for energy and unusual dreams. A
      crock of chili should be kept alongside the
      bed, to be dipped into whenever you get
      sleepy. Don't worry about the after effects.
      The additional carbon dioxide will be good
      for your plants.

Cheesecake (per forkful) 24
      Many consider cheesecake to be an orgasm
      unto itself and frequently use it as a
      partner substitute. Although there is
      significant controversy over the merits of
      Italian versus French cheesecake, we
      suggest both.

Westphalian smoked ham (per thin slice) 11
      The erotic counterpart of baloney. It is
      generally served wrapped around either a
      slice of chilled honeydew or your finger.

Cold seafood salad (per large spoonful) 18
      The perfect fuel for warm-weather sex. It is
      light, nourishing and, if you eat enough,
      acceptably filling.

Potato pancakes (per bite)...........................25
One of the less epicurean of the bedroom
foods, but essential for roughage and
building strength—it is a favorite dish of
Jewish field hands. Those who have
difficulty keeping warm will find potato
pancakes a blessing. Once swallowed, they
burn like peat, enabling one to easily
maintain normal body temperature during
sex in a walk-in freezer.

Chocolate-chip cookies (per bite) 8
By no means intended as a total dietary
program. However, thirty-five
chocolate-chip cookies stored under the
pillow and "popped" at appropriate times
will serve to maintain a proper balance
between the red and white blood cells.
Most healthful type of chocolate-chip
cookies are those made by a caring mother,
or, if one is not available, a doting aunt.
During emergencies, store-purchased
cookies will do.

Wine (per sip)......................................10

The rule here is simplicity itself. White with a thin partner, red with a heavy partner, rosé with a bore. As for serving wine with food, make up your own rules, depending on your own taste and the ignorance of your partner. You'll find that most wines with a grape base go with almost any kind of food. A chilled Chablis, for example, will work just as well with meat loaf as it will with gefilte fish. We do advise, however, against muscatel with oysters Rockefeller and Manischewitz with pork cutlets.

Beer:

(per sip).......................................8
(per gulp) 14

Ice cold beer is a dependable antidote to long, grueling hours of hot, sweaty sex. An ideal way to replace vital body fluids, beer is also rich in vitamins, minerals and carbon dioxide. For extra nutritive power, try dark beer, copious doses of which will give you the strength to sit up and eat. Beer stands up especially well to such formidable dishes as saddle of lamb, chili con carne, hot dogs *en gelée,* goulash and any type of sausage.

Champagne (per tight little sip) 8
     Depending upon taste, pocketbook and how
     you feel about your partner, you can opt for
     anything from a $1.99 bottle of Cold Duck to
     a $15.99 bottle of Taittinger. Champagne
     for bedroom consumption should not be
     restricted to "luxury" foods such as caviar
     and chili. Piper Heidseck served with meat
     loaf has been known to alleviate frigidity
     and Mumm's with yams is a popular
     calmative for those upset by inadequate
     foreplay.

Perrier mineral water 0
     Known in some circles as the perfect water
     substitute, this gently gaseous, highly
     cultured liquid can be taken straight, with
     a twist of lemon, or even beefed up with a
     shot of Yoo Hoo. Perrier can be
     additionally fortified with two parts
     Kool-Aid.

Sodas (sweetened, per swallow) 14
     If carbonated beverage abuse is your thing,
     we suggest the Bordeaux of sodas, Royal
     Crown Cola for its rich, eye-watering flavor
     and polished elegance. If Royal Crown isn't
     available in your area, try Pepsi-Cola, a bit
     thinner but a dependable choice. Soda
     should be uncapped and allowed to stand
     for at least two minutes before serving.

Typical Effects of Alcohol on Bedroom Behavior*

One ounce of alcohol. Little effect. Head still clear, breath not bad. Pulse, breathing and liver normal. Can still satisfy partner.

Two to three ounces. Still pretty much know what you're there for but it somehow doesn't matter. You're growing relaxed, almost tranquil. You don't complain when partner tries to sell you a raffle ticket. Sense of humor still crisp. Fashioning a monocle by holding a cookie to your eye strikes you as unbearably funny.

Four ounces. Minor problem differentiating between bed and floor. Hope partner doesn't notice. Growing feeling of queasiness vanishes when you take a meatball. Changing position brings it back, however, and you suddenly become sick. Partner is gracious and pretends not to notice. Curious urge to boil the bed.

Five to six ounces. Still in control, but ability to perform simple sexual tasks such as drooling and moaning impeded by blinding headache. One of you had an orgasm a few moments ago but you can't remember who. Vision and tactile sensitivity slightly distorted. Cannot locate partner except by listening for a voice. By now you are belching uncontrollably and the dog is cowering in the corner.

Eight to nine ounces. Tongue feels like luncheon meat. Though functionally dead, you find the concept of playing a wind instrument by holding it up to a fan profoundly fascinating. Unaware that partner has departed, you begin a heated argument with the pillow over who should go for ice cream.

*From *New Perspectives on the Relationship Between Alcohol and Silly Behavior,* by Dr. Erica Einstein, Professor of Home Economics, University of the Transvaal.

Examples of Weight Lost While Eating

Activity	Calories burned

Hunger pangs ....½

Opening refrigerator door 1

Shuffling through nonessentials (celery, jelly, egg, lemons, flashlight batteries, etc.) 2

Raising fork containing:
    Good, solid meatball............................4
    Stringy piece of boiled chicken 2
    Italian cheesecake 16
    Consommé 00.000006

Prying lid from inadequately thawed pint of ice cream (includes mangled fingernails) 21

Sliding spoon into:
    Ice cream thawed to creamy consistency 2
    (only the gentlest of pressure should be needed, let gravity do the rest)
    Ice cream just taken from freezer 76
    (includes turning red and panting)
Unbending spoon 6

Note: If you cannot wait for ice cream to melt, use the "shovel" method and stand on the spoon. This will drive the spoon in far enough to give you enough leverage to dislodge an "emergency" portion.

Spreading peanut butter on bread 3

Dipping bread into jar and scooping out peanut butter...1

Separating the halves of an Oreo Creme Sandwich cookie without breaking them 4

Licking off the creme 2

Removing cork from wine bottle:
    With corkscrew 7
    Violent sucking 145
    Hitting bottom of bottle with heel of hand 65

Chewing (per chew):
    Foods such as applesauce, salads, soups 1
    Cheap cuts of meat 11
    Caramel 14

Dialing for a pizza...................................3
Touch-toning for a pizza 1½
Pacing until it arrives 9

Eating pizza:
    Slice folded 4
    Not folded 25
Sucking on pizza tin until it buckles (extreme
hunger) 98

Removing tinfoil from Hershey Kisses 1

Removing wrapper from any candy bar:
    Gently, with fingers 1
    Tearing it off with teeth ....½
    Burning it off ....¼

Trimming the fat from fish 2

Running to catch slowly-pulling-away Good
Humor truck..40

Eating spaghetti using:
    Spoon and fork 6
    Cupped hands............................. ..15

Weight Lost While Resisting Food

People who insist on rigid dieting, even during sex, will be happy to learn that exercising willpower burns considerable calories. The more tempting the food, of course, the more energy needed to successfully resist.

Activity	**Calories burned**

Resisting:

Apple pie with chocolate ice cream	65
A soft-boiled egg	¼
Lettuce	1
Shrimp in lobster sauce	28
Almond Joy	30
Spaghetti and meatballs	
Homemade	55
From a can	2
Succotash	½
Cheesecake	58
Chocolate cake	72
Shredded wheat	00.00004
Frozen tuna pot pie	4
Ice cream	187
Tootsie Roll	19
Cherry pie	40
Broth	0

Eating in Bed—Problems

Activity	Calories burned
Sticking together	5
Prying yourselves apart	14

Removing food stains from sheet:
Ice cream:
Chocolate 5
Vanilla ....don't worry about it
Red wine.......................................8
Tomato sauce 6
Oil from pizza 11
Ground-in meat 8

Note: Food stains should be regarded as symbols of fun, much like the decals people paste on their automobile windows to show they've been to Disneyland.

Bedsores..5
Moving back and forth on a sheet filled with bread crumbs, peanut shells, cherry pits and potato chips will cause tender skin to become irritated. Always vacuum between courses.

Sharing a bowl of soup during intercourse 80

Alternate Uses of Food

Despite the danger of an allergic reaction, covering each other with food such as peanut butter, whipped cream, hot fudge or lox, then licking it off is an excellent way to save time by combining sex with lunch. For best results, wait until you are both undressed before beginning.

Activity	Calories burned

Licking off:

Honey	4
Strawberry jam	6
Turkey leg	19
Chewing gum	86
Whipped cream	2
Shaving cream (good joke)	46
Grapes	1
Organic makeup	10

IX. The Height Report

How Tall Should the Ideal Sex Partner Be?*

(Women over the age of twelve should add one inch to all measurements)

If you are: You should be:

	Small frame	Medium frame	Large frame
14 to 30 lbs.	2 ft. 1 in.	2 ft. 3 in.	2 ft. 5 in.
31 to 42 lbs.	2 ft. 4 in.	2 ft. 7 in.	3 ft.
43 to 54 lbs.	2 ft. 9 in.	3 ft.	3 ft. 3 in.
55 to 65 lbs.	3 ft. 2 in.	3 ft. 7 in.	4 ft. ½ in.
66 to 77 lbs.	3 ft. 9 in.	4 ft. 1 in.	4 ft. 4 in.
78 to 90 lbs.	4 ft.	4 ft. 4 in.	4 ft. 7 in.
91 to 100 lbs.	4 ft. 5 in.	4 ft. 9 in.	5 ft.
101 to 110 lbs.	4 ft. 10 in.	5 ft. 1 in.	5 ft. 3 in.
111 to 122 lbs.	5 ft.	5 ft. 2 in.	5 ft. 5 in.
123 to 135 lbs.	5 ft. 3 in.	5 ft. 5 in.	5 ft. 7 in.
136 to 147 lbs.	5 ft. 3½ in.	5 ft. 6 in.	5 ft. 9 in.
148 to 160 lbs.	5 ft. 7 in.	5 ft. 9 in.	5 ft. 11 in.
161 to 172 lbs.	5 ft. 8 in.	5 ft. 10 in.	6 ft. ¼ in.
173 to 185 lbs.	5 ft. 9 in.	6 ft.	6 ft. 2 in.
186 to 200 lbs.	5 ft. 10 in.	6 ft. 1 in.	6 ft. 4 in.
201 to 212 lbs.	5 ft. 11 in.	6 ft. 2 in.	6 ft. 5 in.
213 to 225 lbs.	6 ft.	6 ft. 3 in.	6 ft. 7 in.
226 to 240 lbs.	6 ft. 4 in.	6 ft. 6 in.	6 ft. 10 in.
241 to 255 lbs.	6 ft. 7 in.	6 ft. 10 in.	7 ft. 2 in.
256 to 270 lbs.	7 ft. ½ in.	7 ft. 3 in.	7 ft. 7 in.
271 to 285 lbs.	7 ft. 3 in.	7 ft. 7 in.	8 ft.

*Based on certain tables.